The |

by Bill Fyffe Hendrie

Lang**Syne**

PUBLISHING

WRITING *to* REMEMBER

Lang**Syne**

PUBLISHING

WRITING *to* REMEMBER

Strathclyde Business Centre
120 Carstairs Street, Glasgow G40 4JD
Tel: 0141 554 9944 Fax: 0141 554 9955
E-mail: info@scottish-memories.co.uk
www.langsyneshop.co.uk

Design by Dorothy Meikle
Printed by Thomson Litho, East Kilbride
© Lang Syne Publishers Ltd 2007
ISBN 1-85217-034-4
ISBN 978-1-85217-034-9

The Buchanans

SEPT NAMES INCLUDE:

Colman	Macauslan
Cormack	MacCalmont
Dewar	MacCormack
Dow	MacGibbon
Gibb	MacInally
Gibson	MacKinlay
Gilbert	MacMaster
Harper	Masters
Macalman	Masterson

The Buchanans

MOTTO:
Brighter Hence The Honour.

CREST:
A Right Hand Holding up a Velvet
and Ermine Cap tassled with a Red Rose
all Within Laurel leaves Proper.

TERRITORY:
Loch Lomondside and Perthshire.

Chapter one:

The origins of the clan system

by Rennie McOwan

The original Scottish clans of the Highlands and the great families of the Lowlands and Borders were gatherings of families, relatives, allies and neighbours for mutual protection against rivals or invaders.

Scotland experienced invasion from the Vikings, the Romans and English armies from the south. The Norman invasion of what is now England also had an influence on land-holding in Scotland. Some of these invaders stayed on and in time became 'Scottish'.

The word clan derives from the Gaelic language term 'clann', meaning children, and it was first used many centuries ago as communities were formed around tribal lands in glens and mountain fastnesses.

The format of clans changed over the centuries, but at its best the chief and his family held the land on behalf of all, like trustees, and the ordinary clansmen and women believed they had a blood relationship with the founder of their clan.

There were two way duties and obligations. An inadequate chief could be deposed and replaced by someone of greater ability.

Clan people had an immense pride in race. Their relationship with the chief was like adult children to a father and they had a real dignity.

The concept of clanship is very old and a more feudal notion of authority gradually crept in.

Pictland, for instance, was divided into seven principalities ruled by feudal leaders who were the strongest and most charismatic leaders of their particular groups.

By the sixth century the 'British' kingdoms of Strathclyde, Lothian and Celtic Dalriada (Argyll) had emerged and Scotland, as one nation, began to take shape in the time of King Kenneth MacAlpin.

Some chiefs claimed descent from

ancient kings which may not have been accurate in every case.

By the twelfth and thirteenth centuries the clans and families were more strongly brought under the central control of Scottish monarchs.

Lands were awarded and administered more and more under royal favour, yet the power of the area clan chiefs was still very great.

The long wars to ensure Scotland's independence against the expansionist ideas of English monarchs extended the influence of some clans and reduced the lands of others.

Those who supported Scotland's greatest king, Robert the Bruce, were awarded the territories of the families who had opposed his claim to the Scottish throne.

In the Scottish Borders country - the notorious Debatable Lands - the great families built up a ferocious reputation for providing warlike men accustomed to raiding into England and occasionally fighting one another.

Chiefs had the power to dispense justice

and to confiscate lands and clan warfare produced a society where martial virtues - courage, hardiness, tenacity - were greatly admired.

Gradually the relationship between the clans and the Crown became strained as Scottish monarchs became more orientated to life in the Lowlands and, on occasion, towards England.

The Highland clans spoke a different language, Gaelic, whereas the language of Lowland Scotland and the court was Scots and in more modern times, English.

Highlanders dressed differently, had different customs, and their wild mountain land sometimes seemed almost foreign to people living in the Lowlands.

It must be emphasised that Gaelic culture was very rich and story-telling, poetry, piping, the clarsach (harp) and other music all flourished and were greatly respected.

Highland culture was different from other parts of Scotland but it was not inferior or less sophisticated.

Central Government, whether in London

"The spirit of the clan means much to thousands of people"

or Edinburgh, sometimes saw the Gaelic clans as a challenge to their authority and some sent expeditions into the Highlands and west to crush the power of the Lords of the Isles.

Nevertheless, when the eighteenth century Jacobite Risings came along the cause of the Stuarts was mainly supported by Highland clans.

The word Jacobite comes from the Latin for James - Jacobus. The Jacobites wanted to restore the exiled Stuarts to the throne of Britain.

The monarchies of Scotland and England became one in 1603 when King James VI of Scotland (1st of England) gained the English throne after Queen Elizabeth died.

The Union of Parliaments of Scotland and England, the Treaty of Union, took place in 1707.

Some Highland clans, of course, and Lowland families opposed the Jacobites and supported the incoming Hanoverians.

After the Jacobite cause finally went down at Culloden in 1746 a kind of ethnic cleansing took place. The power of the chiefs was curtailed. Tartan and the pipes were banned in law.

Many emigrated, some because they wanted to, some because they were evicted by force. In addition, many Highlanders left for the cities of the south to seek work.

Many of the clan lands became home to sheep and deer shooting estates.

But the warlike traditions of the clans and the great Lowland and Border families lived on, with their descendants fighting bravely for freedom in two world wars.

Remember the men from whence you came, says the Gaelic proverb, and to that could be added the role of many heroic women.

The spirit of the clan, of having roots, whether Highland or Lowland, means much to thousands of people.

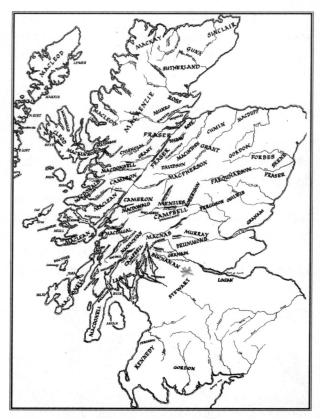

A map of the clans' homelands

Chapter two:

The battle cry "Clarinch"

"Clarinch", the battle cry of the Buchanans, comes from the name of the small island in Loch Lomond, along whose eastern shore the clan's lands originally clustered.

According to tradition these lands came into the possession of the Buchanans as a result of a grant from the Earl of Lennox in the year 1225 to one Absalom. He is thought to have been a priest, as the name Buchanan is derived from the Gaelic "buth channain" meaning "the house of the canon".

Towards the end of the same century in 1282, a later Earl of Lennox granted a charter confirming Morris Buchanan as a chief of the clan and also his baronial rights to the lands on the shores of Scotland's largest inland loch. The power and wealth of the Buchanans increased and clan possessions soon spread to the east and to the north of the famous loch across what became known as Stirlingshire.

By the start of the 14th century the Chief of the Buchanans was active in the fight to establish Scotland as an independent country and in 1314 he supported King Robert the Bruce at the Battle of Bannockburn and helped bring him victory over King Edward II and his English troops.

In turn the Buchanans' backing for the Bruce was rewarded with royal favours and the family flourished throughout the remainder of the century.

As one of Scotland's most important nobles, Sir Alexander Buchanan travelled to France in the year 1421 along with other leading Scottish lords to lend their support to the French, in the best traditions of the famous Auld Alliance, in the fight against the common enemy, the English.

In the Battle of Beauge in Normandy against the army of King Henry V, Alexander Buchanan showed outstanding courage and succeeded in slaying the English Duke of Clarence. As he rode off in triumph he raised high Clarence's ducal cap, which is to this day depicted atop the Buchanan family crest.

Alexander's successor, Sir William Buchanan, married the only daughter of Murdoch, Duke of Albany, third son of King Robert II. The duke had been regent during the minority of King James I. When he died in 1420 the role of regent passed to his only son, a man whose conduct and lawlessness made him deeply unpopular. After the young king came to power in his own right, this regent Buchanan was executed by beheading in 1425. Thus his heirs lost all rights and became disinherited. The unusual black fleur de lis in the Buchanan coat of arms is said to bemourn this loss of status.

Despite being deprived of this royal connection the Buchanans continued to exert much influence over their Stirlingshire territories and the members of the branch of the family who lived at Arnprior near Scotland's only lake, the Lake of Menteith, were so powerful and influential that they earned for themselves the title of the Kings of Kippen, a name derived from the nearest town.

It was at their thick, grey, stone-walled,

fortified tower house or keep at Arnprior that the Buchanans enjoyed a royal visit, the details of which have become part of the lore of the family, because of its unusual nature. In the middle of the 15th century, King James V became known as a monarch much in touch with his royal subjects and the way in which he got to know so much about the life of the common people was by he himself travelling incognito as a commoner.

On these sometimes dangerous journeys he always used the same nickname of the Guid Man O' Ballengeich. One dark stormy night, knowing that the Buchanans were famed for keeping a good table, King Jamie decided to spend the night in the shelter of their home and arrived unannounced at the door of the keep at Arnprior. Annoyed at being disturbed on such a miserably nasty, wet night His Majesty received the surliest of welcomes from the servant who answered the door. The servant was, however, at last persuaded to bear the news upstairs to his master in the hall above where he announced that the Guid Man O' Ballengeich had come to call.

When he heard the name of Ballengeich, Buchanan immediately recognised it and realised that he and his family had been honoured by a royal visit. Sweeping the servant aside he dashed down the twisting, spiral, turnpike stairs to usher the King up to the warmth of the hall, where the generous and very genuine hospitality soon made up for the dourness of the original welcome.

The Buchanans' loyal support for the Scottish royal family continued throughout the 16th century and in 1547 it cost the clan chief his life when he was killed fighting against the English invaders at the Battle of Pinkie at Musselburgh in 1547.

It was shortly after this that one of the most famous members of the clan, George Buchanan made his name first as an advisor to Mary Queen of Scots and later as tutor to her only son James, the future King James VI, who later by the Union of the Crowns in the year 1603 also became James I of England.

Chapter three:

Tutor to the King

"More remarkable for its antiquity than its opulence", is how George Buchanan described the family into which he was born in 1506. He was born very much in the heart of the clan lands near Killearn in Stirlingshire and despite his parents' lack of wealth received a good basic education. This he built upon thanks to the generosity of one of his Buchanan uncles who paid for him to study first at university in Paris and later back in Scotland at the University of St. Andrews, where he studied philosophy.

Buchanan returned to France to complete his university education and after graduating in Paris found work as tutor to the Earl of Cassilis. By the time he returned to Scotland again, his reputation as an able schoolmaster led to his appointment by King James V as dominie at the royal court at Holyrood Palace in Edinburgh.

As well as coaching the young princes at

their Latin and other lessons, King James demanded that Buchanan should turn his hand to play writing and produce a political satire against the brothers of the Franciscan Order, who the king was convinced were conspiring against him. The biting drama was duly staged at the royal court to the delight of the king, but to the even greater fury of Scotland's leading churchman, Cardinal Beaton, who captured Buchanan and imprisoned him in his stronghold, St. Andrew's Castle, high on its clifftop site, overlooking the North Sea.

Despite the castle's formidable defences, Buchanan succeeded in escaping and sought safety in France, where he became a Professor at the University of Bordeaux. His fame as an academic spread and he was invited by the King of Portugal to become Professor of Philosophy at the University of Coimbra in 1547. His move to Portugal was however an unfortunate one because it led to his involvement with the infamous Inquisition and two years later in 1549 he was imprisoned again, this time as a heretic to the Roman Catholic church. It says much for his faith that when he was released after two years in captivity, he then spent the next decade in Italy and France studying religion in order to better understand the controversies which raged at the time of the Reformation.

When at last he returned once more to Scotland it was as a convinced Protestant, but when he was made Latin advisor to the still loyally Roman Catholic Mary Queen of Scots, he became a dedicated supporter of the unhappy monarch, until the murder at Kirk o' Field in Edinburgh of her second husband, her cousin, Lord Henry Darnley, in which Buchanan was convinced she was implicated, although this was never proved.

By this time Buchanan was one of the most powerful men in the country and in 1570 he was made Keeper of the Privy Seal, a position which entitled him to a seat in the Scottish Parliament. By then he was an elderly, confirmed bachelor so it seems strange that in the same year he was also chosen to become tutor to Mary Queen of Scots' four year old son and heir, the future King James VI and I.

Throughout his two previous terms as a schoolmaster, Buchanan had gained an awesome reputation as a disciplinarian, whose Bible readings had apparently thoroughly convinced him that Solomon was correct when he said that to spare the rod was to spoil the child. The earliest written mention of the word tawse, the Scottish name for the long, lithe leather thronged strap with which for centuries Scottish dominies chastised their pupils, occurs in a list of contents for the royal palace at Linlithgow, at the time when Buchanan was teaching the children of King James V and his second wife, the French Mary of Guise.

Entrusted now with the education of the little Prince James, Buchanan determined that the fact that his pupil was the heir to the throne should not save him from physical corrective treatment. Normally any corporal punishments earned by the heir to the throne were administered instead to a little page, who had the dubious honour of being royal whipping boy, but Buchanan dispensed with this refinement and became famed for the thrashings which he meted out to the prince, on the gorunds that the quickest way to impart Latin grammar to young James' brain was through his bottom. The education, which Buchanan provided for the future King was described at the time as "brilliant but brutal".

Perhaps even more seriously he was also accused of using his position as tutor to poison James' mind against his mother. It was said that Buchanan even withheld the toys, which Queen Mary sent to her son from her English prison. There is no doubt that Buchanan's education of James helped turn him into what was described as "the wisest fool in Christendom."

His task of teaching the future king completed, George Buchanan devoted the rest of his life to writing, including an important work denouncing the old belief in the divine right of kings and the first truly comprehensive history of Scotland.

This very learned member of the Buchanan family died in Edinburgh in 1582 and was buried in the city's Greyfriars' Churchyard.

Chapter four:

Making their mark

The Clan Buchanan was dealt a severe blow in 1682 when the chief passed away without an heir and the principal line of the family thus died out.

Even before then the family was deeply in debt. Most of their lands were therefore sold off to pay their debtors and what remained passed to the Marquis of Montrose. This was particularly galling for the Buchanans as their fortunes had earlier benefited from the disgrace of their neighbour James Graham, Marquis of Montrose.

Now however the Buchanans had to sell out to his successor and suffer the humiliation of watching the Dukes of Montrose move from Mugdock Castle to the House of Buchanan, which they subsequently replaced with a much larger and grander stately home. Adding further insult to injury, the Montrose family named their magnificent new home, Buchanan Castle. It was built by

William Burn, the Edinburgh architect, who was the master of Scottish country house design. Today, even as a ruin, it remains impressive.

During this difficult time for the Buchanans many emigrated to Ulster to try to improve their lot. While some stayed in Ireland, others moved still further away from Scotland and sailed across the Atlantic to make new lives for themselves in America. Most famous descendant of this branch of the Buchanan family was James Buchanan, who was born in Mercersburg, Pennsylvania in 1792 and went on to become President of the United States of America, when he was elected as Democratic Party candidate in 1856.

For a time during the 18th and early part of the 19th century Clan Buchanan was without a chieftain, but its clansfolk remained active and prominent in Scottish life.

The Clan boasts the oldest clan society in the world. The Buchanan Society was established in Glasgow in 1725. Its first chairman was George Buchanan who was described in the original records as a maltman, meaning a brewer. His successor was Patrick Buchanan, who was one of the city's prosperous merchants. All members of the Buchanan Society had to make annual contributions to its funds, which were kept in a sturdy large locked wooden box. The first treasurer or box master as he was known was John Buchanan, who was a maltman or brewer. The considerable wealth which accured in the box was used to pay the fees of boys of the name Buchanan to ensure that they received the best possible education.

When they grew up, many of the boys became successful city businessmen and in their turn nurtured the funds of the Buchanan Society so that future generations also benefited. One of the best known Buchanans of this period was one of Glasgow's celebrated Tobacco Lords, James Buchanan, who made a fortune importing raw tobacco from Virginia and other British colonies and re-exporting it to the Netherlands, where the Dutch turned it into fine cigars.

A Glasgow city landmark known to both natives and visitors alike is the tower of the Buchanan Whisky headquarters on the eastern outskirts at Stepps. James Buchanan became a whisky merchant in London in 1884. From this small beginning the famous company grew. The Buchanan company later merged with Dewars of Perth and in 1925 became part of the Distillers Company. Buchanan's Black and White Whisky, traditionally advertised by two wee black and white West Highland terrier dogs, is still a favourite brand of blended Scotch worldwide.

As well as commerce, Buchanans have over the centuries also made their mark in many other aspects of Scottish life. Dugald Buchanan of Rannoch in Perthshire, is generally known as Scotland's finest Gaelic evangelical poet. He wrote a particularly vivid and dramatic account of the day of judgement. His other works include "Winter" and "The Warrior". He was born in 1716 and died in 1768.

Another Buchanan who influenced development of religion though in a different manner was the Rev. Robert Buchanan. Born in 1802 he was one of the leaders of the break up of the Church of Scotland in 1843, because of his belief that congregations should have the right to choose their own minister rather than having one chosen for them by the local laird. He took part in the walk out of ministers at the General Assembly in Edinburgh and went on to help found the new Free Church of Scotland. His book on the Disruption, became the accepted text about these events, which continue to affect Scottish church life to the present day.

While Victorian times marked changes in opinion in the church, it was also a period of change of thought in politics and Robert Wilson Buchanan, the son of a new Glasgow publisher expressed the new socialist views, which he inherited from his father, in his novels, plays and other writings. He also wrote poetry of which "North Coast" is a fine example. After moving south to London, his 'London Poems', published in 1866 became his most successful collection.

At the same time another Buchanan was working to try to improve the lot of the capital's poorest citizens. He was Dr. George Buchanan who was appointed Medical Officer for the city's

St Giles district, which contained the capital's worst slums. So notorious was the name St. Giles that King George III refused to allow it to be used for the name of one of the main thoroughfares in the Georgian New Town of Edinburgh, preferring instead to call it Princess Street. A century later in Dr. Buchanan's day conditions in Victorian St. Giles were even worse as overcrowding had increased despite the district having the country's highest mortality rate. Dr. Buchanan did much to improve sanitary conditions, but sadly carried home the infectious and contagious diseases of the slums, which resulted in the deaths of both his wife and young son. These tragic events made Buchanan even more determined to improve the health of the people and he was commissioned by the government to write an official report on insanitary conditions and the measures necessary to improve conditions. He was also a leading campaigner for the Compulsory Vaccination Act and was knighted for his medical and social work.

During this century Buchanans who have brought distinction to the family name range from the debonair Jack Buchanan from Helensburgh, who with his black top hat, white ties, tails and silver topped cane was such a star of stage and screen musicals of the thirties and forties, to Edinburgh born Kenny Buchanan, who became World Light Weight Boxing Champion. Buchanan won his title when he defeated Ismael Laguna in San Juan, Puerto Rico, in 1970. Many still regard Buchanan as the finest boxer Scotland has ever produced.

At the beginning of the 1970's a prosperous member of Clan Buchanan purchased Clarinch, the little island in Loch Lomond, which has always meant so much to the clan and donated it to members. Clarinch has now been turned into a nature reserve, a peaceful role in marked contrast to the name of the island's previous use as a war cry and rallying call of the clan.

Inch is the Gaelic word for an island and another of the lovely little inches in Loch Lomond, which has a very special place in the history of Clan Buchanan, is Inchcailleach. It lies just off the shore at Balmaha and was originally the tranquil setting for a Celtic nunnery. It is there that several of the Buchanan clan chiefs lie buried.

Members of the Buchanan family who return on pilgrimages to these lands of their forebears will find much to interest them from cruising by motor launch from Balloch, Luss or Tarbert around the islands of Loch Lomond, which is the largest stretch of inland water in Britain, to visiting Killearn to admire the memorial to George Buchanan, the royal dominie. It was erected on the village green by the Buchanan Society in 1788.

Principle lines of the Buchanan family today are Buchanans of Arnprior, the Buchanan of Auchmar, the Buchanans of Carbeth, the Buchanans of Drumakill and the Buchanans of Leny.